Under The Stars

A Comedy

Richard Crane

A Samuel French Acting Edition

SAMUELFRENCH-LONDON.CO.UK
SAMUELFRENCH.COM

Copyright © 1994 by Richard Crane
All Rights Reserved

UNDER THE STARS is fully protected under the copyright laws of the British Commonwealth, including Canada, the United States of America, and all other countries of the Copyright Union. All rights, including professional and amateur stage productions, recitation, lecturing, public reading, motion picture, radio broadcasting, television and the rights of translation into foreign languages are strictly reserved.

ISBN 978-0-573-01911-1

www.samuelfrench-london.co.uk

www.samuelfrench.com

FOR AMATEUR PRODUCTION ENQUIRIES

UNITED KINGDOM AND WORLD EXCLUDING NORTH AMERICA

plays@SamuelFrench-London.co.uk

020 7255 4302/01

Each title is subject to availability from Samuel French, depending upon country of performance.

CAUTION: Professional and amateur producers are hereby warned that UNDER THE STARS is subject to a licensing fee. Publication of this play does not imply availability for performance. Both amateurs and professionals considering a production are strongly advised to apply to the appropriate agent before starting rehearsals, advertising, or booking a theatre. A licensing fee must be paid whether the title is presented for charity or gain and whether or not admission is charged.

The professional rights in this play are controlled by Casarotto Ramsay & Associates Ltd, Waverley House, 7-12 Noel Street, London, W1F 8GQ.

No one shall make any changes in this title for the purpose of production. No part of this book may be reproduced, stored in a retrieval system, or transmitted in any form, by any means, now known or yet to be invented, including mechanical, electronic, photocopying, recording, videotaping, or otherwise, without the prior written permission of the publisher. No one shall upload this title, or part of this title, to any social media websites.

The right of Richard Crane to be identified as author of this work has been asserted by him in accordance with Section 77 of the Copyright, Designs and Patents Act 1988

UNDER THE STARS

First produced at Greenwich Theatre, London, on 22 July 1993 with the following cast:

Stella	Connie Booth
Regina	Pam Ferris
Charles	Tyler Butterworth
P.Q.	Nicholas Gecks
The Known Actress	Penny Morrell

and the voices of

The Dame	Patricia Routledge
Trixie	June Whitfield

Directed by Matthew Francis
Designed by Lez Brotherston
Lighting by Kevin Sleep

The action of the play takes place in the Understudies' dressing-room

Time: the present

ACT I

Scene 1

Two spots pick out Stella and Regina downstage, in black shawls and black rehearsal skirts. They are rehearsing Helen's arrival, after years of wandering, at the house of Clytemnestra

Stella/Helen Knowst thou my face, the fairest face on earth?
 Helen am I and thou my long lost sister
 Clytemnestra.
Regina/Clytemnestra   Age hath trick'd thy visage.
 I perceive no likeness, no nor liking
 in this untrue and unwelcome face.
Stella/Helen Cast back thy mind before the war with Troy.
 Twin cradled babes were we, as loved and loving
 as two doves—
Regina/Clytemnestra   As hawks whose warring talons
 destin'd were to tear men's flesh—
Stella/Helen   My doves,
 thy hawks, thou *dost* remember!
Regina/Clytemnestra   No, I'll not—
Stella/Helen Recall—
Regina/Clytemnestra Ah let me not recall—
Stella/Helen   . . . as children,
 how all day we played—
Regina/Clytemnestra   . . . long hateful days
 in long cold hateful halls—
Stella/Helen   . . . in our dear father's
 house—
Regina/Clytemnestra . . . longing to be free from a sister's
 treachery and games.
Stella/Helen   No treachery now,
 though many a game there'll be if thou vouchsaf'st

Regina/Clytemnestra Vouchsafe me death!
Stella/Helen . . . in th'autumn of my days
   to clasp these knees! (*She falls at Clytemnestra's feet*)
Regina/Clytemnestra   Begone!
Stella/Helen   Oh sister mine,
   ten years it is—
Regina/Clytemnestra   Begone I say!
Stella/Helen   . . . since I
   was torn from Troy, ten tearful tortured years
   of vainly hoping with each spring to melt . . .
   my loveless . . . stiff-neck'd . . . sister's . . . heart . . .
   (*She suddenly freezes*)

Light has gradually come up on the understudies' dressing-room: a cluttered but comfortable home from home. Mirrors framed with light-bulbs, photos, cards, make-up tins, knitting and shopping bags, magazines, kettle and mugs; chipped basin with practical taps, costume rail, folding screen or curtain, old easy chair, folding chairs, chaise-longue

Charles, upstage, is directing the scene, with stop-watch and the book

There is a pause

Charles Come on Stella. We're timing this.

Pause

Regina Is it the Method again, Stella?
Stella (*as in a trance*) We're going to fold, I know it. We're closing. A few weeks, a month, two months, I can feel it. This play—Oh God—it's going to close . . .
Charles We're nearly full tonight, and booking through to July.
Regina The box office is really not your problem Stella.
Stella So little time . . . so little *time* . . .
Charles Let's make use of it then, shall we? Ten years . . .? Come on love . . .
Stella/Helen Ten years it is—
Regina/Clytemnestra   Begone I say!
Stella (*breaking down*) I'm sorry I'm sorry I'm sorry I'm sorry . . .
Charles Are you not well, Stella?
Stella I'm all right.

Regina She's all right.
Stella I'm sorry.
Regina And she's sorry.
Stella I don't know what it is. It possesses me! I'm sorry, truly sorry. I'm sorry Charles. Sorry . . . I'm sorry . . .
Regina If you say sorry again, I shall squeak.
Stella Sorry?

Regina squeaks

Charles (*approaching Stella*) Stella love—
Stella Don't touch me! It's not *me*. It's something *in* me. It's the part. It's something *in* Helen. Her divinity!—because she was fathered by Zeus himself, unlike Clytemnestra—
Regina . . . who was just a housewife.
Stella It's in the words, something . . . mystical. It . . . triggers a nerve . . .
Charles Can you control this nerve Stella? It's just that we are a teeny bit pushed for time.
Stella A *teeny* bit!
Charles I mean rehearsal time.
Stella Life is not a rehearsal. Who said that? Life is not a rehearsal. Who was it?
Regina Pass.
Stella (*eyes closed, concentrating*) Helen of Troy. It was her motto. Her epitaph—except she was fated never to die. The whole world might die but she would *live*. She *is* life. It's in every line she speaks.
Regina When she gets round to speaking.
Stella There's no "rehearsing" in life when you're Helen, Regina. It's the real thing. She's a star! All her world's a stage! She only *lives* on stage. That's why I'm finding all this (*she breaks down*) so impossible, so perplexing. Who am I? What am I?
Charles You're an understudy—
Stella I am Helen. She demands it. And yet I can't be, because Trixie is Helen and I have to be Trixie *being* Helen, but that's so dishonest, so contrary to what Helen *is*, I can't *become* her, I can't extricate myself.
Regina Have you tried acting?
Stella (*icily*) Oh how simple, Regina. That's the answer. How silly of me. Let's pretend. Let's cheat.

Regina I think she's feeling better now.
Charles Vouchsafe . . .
Regina/Clytemnestra Vouchsafe me death!
Stella/Helen   . . . in th'autumn of my days
   to clasp these knees . . .
Charles Trixie does go down here Stella, in two sort of jerky movements, with the upstage arm sort of raised.
Stella Yes, I know.
Charles Could you do it then?
Stella Yes, I could.
Charles Would you then? We are pushed—
Stella I *could* go down in twenty-seven epileptic *spasms*—
Charles I'm not asking—
Stella You can't throw Helen at me Charles. I'm a professional, and whatever one's "company status", one does have a responsibility to one's role. I *am* Helen. I *am* Trixie. I *am* Stella Widgery. I signed a contract. It's my professional responsibility to pick my way through the jungle and I *will* find a way. Of course I will, I'm trained. I will, I *will* get there . . .
Regina But *when* will you get there?
Charles Reg does have a point Stella.
Stella Can we have some space? (*Thrusting and throwing aside furniture and props*) There's no room here!
Charles (*prompting*) No treachery now . . .?
Stella How can anybody be expected to rehearse in a dressing-room?
Charles "Though many a game there'll be . . ." Come on love . . . "If thou vouchsaf'st . . ."
Regina/Clytemnestra Vouchsafe me death!
Charles Down, Stella, down.
Stella/Helen   (*kneeling*) . . . in th'autumn of my days
   to clasp these knees—
Regina/Clytemnestra   Begone!
Stella/Helen   Oh sister dear,
   ten years it is—
Regina/Clytemnestra Begone I say!
Stella/Helen   Since I
   (*Slowly*) was torn . . . from . . . Troy . . .
Charles Trixie takes this a bit faster Stella.
Stella/Helen (*slower*) . . . ten . . . teeearful . . . toooortured . . . yeeeears . . .

Act I, Scene 1

No that's wrong.
Regina You're right.
Stella It's not right . . .
Regina It's wrong.
Stella (*crying*) I've got to know why I'm crying . . .
Regina You're crying because Trixie is crying.
Stella Why is Trixie crying?
Charles Ours not to reason why . . .
Regina Ours but to give copy-cat performances and not dry.
Stella I find that attitude so *craven*. I'm sorry. And don't say we're lucky to be employed.
Regina We're lucky to be employed.
Stella I happen to believe we are as vital to the theatre as the very lights!
Regina We are the spare bulbs.
Stella As vital, yes, as the spare bulbs!
Regina Spare, low wattage, economy price . . . bulbs.
Charles So let's shine, shall we loves, bright as we can . . .?
Stella Could I say just one thing? Then I'll shut up.
Regina Promise?
Stella I promise.
Regina Just one thing.
Stella Well it's two actually.
Regina No, one. You promised.
Stella Well I won't say anything then.
Charles Right!
Stella I just want to know when P.Q. is coming to see us, because I want an assurance about what will really happen when Trixie and the Dame are *off*, as well they might be. They're both bronchial and Trixie, poor love, has a heart condition—
Charles If either or both of them are off, then you're on.
Stella I want an assurance—
Charles I'm giving you one—
Stella That they won't just close the show, give people their money back.
Charles They wouldn't do that.
Regina They might.
Charles They couldn't, Reg love.
Regina But they just might, Charles dear.
Stella I want to be sure of that.

Charles I'll put the point to P.Q.

Stella I want him to tell us in person. I want him to come and see us.

Regina Why?

Stella Because he is the director, Regina.

Charles He is most frightfully busy, Stella.

Stella He's never yet once been to see us. He must think we're not committed to going on and we'll just capitulate and accept it when they close the show. He must think we're just here to clock in and clock out and we don't *want* him.

Regina We don't. We have Charles. Charles is our director. Aren't you Charles?

Charles (*clapping*) Can we rehearse please, loves?

Stella Charles has no authority.

Charles (*with authority*) Can we rehearse loves *please*!

Stella Poor P.Q. I saw him in his office on my way up. He looked so wretched, he didn't even smile when I caught his eye. I was so ashamed. He looked *drained*, as if he couldn't understand why everyone is so afraid of simply rising to his challenge. He really is not God Almighty you know. He's young enough to be one's child. (*She goes to the door*) I'm going to see him.

Charles (*blocking the door*) If anyone's going to see P.Q. it will be me. After rehearsal.

Stella We want him to *come* to rehearsal.

Regina I don't want anyone at rehearsal till we've had a rehearsal.

Stella I'm not rehearsing till I know someone is here who can give me direction, and *notes*. This is a massively demanding, chance-of-a-lifetime part, and I don't know which way to turn . . .

Charles All the turns are marked in the book love.

Stella I haven't been in the business thirty-two years to be fobbed off with a *trainee* director—

Charles *Assistant* director.

Stella I'm sorry Charles, but I haven't. I'm not used to being passed over, ignored . . .

Regina Ignore her.

Stella (*muttering*) Of course you'll be running to him *after* rehearsal. I know you will. "P.Q. we're having a little trouble with Stella. She's not *craven* enough." He'll just laugh—(*She laughs*) He'll say "Thank God there's someone with *chutzpah* in this production". That's his word—*chutzpah*. We talked about it at the audition.

That's why he cast me. He trusts me. He knows that if Trixie—God forbid—drops *dead*, I can be relied upon, not just to parrot her lines, but to hold the stage, to shine! Is that arrogance? Is that *hubris*, ye gods? (*She looks up*) Will the heavens fall . . .?

Pause

Charles While we've stopped, Reg love, the Dame does turn on "loveless stiff-neck'd sister".
Regina She doesn't.
Charles She does.
Regina She does not.
Charles (*showing her*) Let me show you in the book.
Regina I was in last night and she didn't.
Charles She didn't turn?
Regina Didn't budge.
Charles But it says here . . .
Regina The Dame has never turned on "loveless stiff-neck'd sister".
Charles (*erasing and correcting in the book*) Then Holy Writ will have to be amended . . .
Tannoy Announcement This is your half an hour call. Half an hour please, ladies and gentlemen.
Charles And the inflection on "games" is a tone lower.
Regina (*in a lower register*) Games.
Charles Like a growl.
Regina (*lower still*) Games.
Charles All right?
Regina Treachery and (*low*) games . . .
Charles All right, Stella love? Let's try and get to the end of Scene One. (*He sighs*) Vainly hoping . . .?
Stella/Helen Vainly hoping with each spring to melt
my loveless stiff-neck'd sister's heart . . .

The Lights fade

Scene 2

A performance is in progress. The voices of Trixie and The Dame are heard over the main speakers

Trixie/Helen Oh sister
let thy lips receive this kiss of spring
which even now warms winter's icy veins.
This iron earth let Nature's key unlock;
this sleeping love the spring of mercy raise.
Dame/Clytemnestra No spring may raise the bones thou hast unflesh'd,
no nature free the free-born damn'd by thee—
Trixie/Helen Yet see the shoots break vicious winter's hold!
Dame/Clytemnestra Thy treach'rous lust a guileless world inflam'd.
Trixie/Helen Bulbs thrust their joyous stems! Birds bust on trees!
Dame/Clytemnestra The flow'r of all our youth thou hast cut down
and burnt in thine accurs'd adult'rous fires . . .!

The sound switches to the onstage tannoy as the Lights come up on the dressing-room. Regina is sitting in the easy chair knitting a large mohair shawl. Stella is sitting poised on the chaise doing breathing exercises

Regina (*turning the tannoy down*) She said it again.
Stella Said what?
Regina And she said it last night. "Birds bust on trees." Instead of "Buds burst—"
Stella It's an easy mistake to make.
Regina You'll have to learn it like that, if it's fixed.
Stella I certainly shall not. When *I* go on as Helen, the last thing Trixie will want is me perpetuating her fluffs.
Regina The last thing Trixie will want is you going on as Helen.

Stella sighs

How are you feeling dear?
Stella On edge.
Regina I expect she's just saying it to annoy. "Birds bust."
Stella Buds burst.
Regina She's so spiteful.
Stella So brave. I so admire her.

Act I, Scene 2   9

Regina Silly cow.
Stella The insults she has to put up with from that ox! And in public! Did you see them on that chat show?
Regina It was carnage.
Stella I couldn't watch it.
Regina Trixie wittering about the Red Dame and her socialist principles and the Dame flattening her every time, like a bulldozer.
Stella They've never got on. People should respect that.
Regina She said how could the Dame claim to be an "actress of the people" when the play she was currently in was incomprehensible to the vast mass of the public who couldn't afford the tickets anyway?
Stella She didn't say that!
Regina She did.
Stella She wouldn't, not Trixie. She's loyal.
Regina That's why she said it. It was a feed, so the Dame could then biff her with a report about regular coach parties of ordinary working Londoners—
Stella They shouldn't force her onto these programmes.
Regina . . . and bop her with slashed seat-prices for pensioners and the unemployed.
Stella She's so frail. It'll be the end of her.
Regina They know what they're doing. It's like a pantomime.
Stella Oh no it's not.
Regina Oh yes it is!
Stella People do not come to see our two première actresses tearing each other to pieces.
Regina Oh yes they do!
Stella They do not! It would close the show.
Regina It's what keeps it going. Haven't you seen them at the box office baying for blood?
Stella Are you asking me to believe when they appear together on television . . .
Regina It's fixed. It's rigged. It's like wrestling.

Pause

Stella The fight! We haven't done the fight.
Regina We did it yesterday dear.
Stella We only marked it.
Regina We learnt the moves.

Stella It's unheard of. A principal actress needs to know what the understudy is like. We should be fighting once a week with our principals.
Regina I've given up fighting with my principles.
Stella P.Q. must be so disappointed. He hasn't been to *one* rehearsal. He must think we don't care. Whatever happened to *chutzpah*?
Regina It wasn't in the budget.
Stella And when are we running on set? It's all steps. I won't go on. And costumes! Have you had a fitting?
Regina Nope.
Stella What are we going to do about it?
Regina I'm knitting mine.

Pause

Stella There's every likelihood we'll have to go on, you know that. They're both well into their seventies. Poor Trixie, I so worry for her. She's had TB. She's thin as a rake. She never eats or sleeps. She's utterly utterly possessed by her art. She *is* Helen and it's killing her.
Regina Said Stella hopefully.
Stella Why do you say things like that Regina?
Regina Because I'm like that. And the name's Reg.
Stella When I first met you I believed your heart was in the theatre.
Regina I was acting.
Stella You don't know the meaning of the word.
Regina What is the meaning of the word?
Stella It means exploring, being truthful, discovering . . .
Regina Oh, so that's what you were doing in rehearsal. I thought you were just spoiling it.
Stella I brought it to life actually.
Regina Understudies aren't meant to bring things to life, except in cases of dire emergency.

Pause

Stella What's that thing you're knitting?
Regina It's a shawl. Do you like it?
Stella It's like a shroud.
Regina It's mohair. (*Counting stitches*) Four, eight, twelve, sixteen . . .
Stella It's sinister. It's making me tense.

Act I, Scene 2   11

Regina . . . twenty . . . twenty-four . . . twenty-eight . . .
Stella This pernicious ritual. You're like those women at the guillotine, waiting for heads to roll.
Regina . . . thirty-six . . . forty . . . forty-four . . . forty-eight . . .
Stella (*annoyingly*) fifty-three . . . eighty-five . . . twenty-one, key of the door . . . all the nines, ninety-nine, legs eleven, on its own number one . . .
Regina Could you find yourself something to do please?
Stella Sorry.
Regina And don't start apologizing.
Stella Sorry sorry.

Pause

(*Suddenly*) The fault dear Brutus is not in our stars, but in our*selves* that we are understudies.
Regina Under*lings*.
Stella You have to *want* it. And all actors do, or they wouldn't be actors. You have to kill for it. Oh yes, we've all got our own little Scottish king inside us, though we won't admit it – certainly not in the dressing-room! Or don't you agree?

Pause

Click-click-clackety-clack!
Regina I don't want blood on my knitting.
Stella It's driving me mad!
Regina But it's for you.
Stella What?
Regina This shawl. It's for you.
Stella For me?
Regina But you don't like it.
Stella I didn't say I didn't like it—
Regina You *do* like it?
Stella (*emotionally*) I don't know. I'm so confused.
Regina Either you like it or you don't like it.
Stella It's the not knowing. I don't know . . . It's the pressure, the waiting. I'm so new to this.
Regina New to what?
Stella All . . . *this.*
Regina You've never acted before?

Stella Oh I've acted! I've acted all my life. My whole *life* has been in acting.
Regina You've never understudied.
Stella I've never been under such pressure . . . to go on . . . as an understudy . . .

Pause

Regina Nor have I.
Stella No, but you've done it.
Regina Done what?
Stella Gone on.
Regina No.
Stella You haven't?
Regina Never.
Stella You've never gone on as an understudy?
Regina I have never gone on as an understudy.
Stella But you've been covering the Dame for—
Regina Twenty-five years.
Stella And you've never had to go on?
Regina Never once.

Pause

Stella Is that true?
Regina As true as I'm sitting here wasting my time knitting you a shawl which you don't want.
Stella I find that so sad. You must feel so unfulfilled.
Regina I'm a deterrent.
Stella I'd be suicidal by now.
Regina I think it's quite an achievement.
Stella I am an actress. I live to act.
Regina I am a stage weight. I live to stop actresses falling over.
Stella You have such a low opinion of yourself, Regina.
Regina Reg.
Stella Regina. It's a royal name. I won't shorten it.

Pause

Tannoy Announcement Stand by, please, for lights down on Act One Scene Two.
Stella When I was just leaving RADA, I went to see a medium, while all the others were off doing bit-part auditions. I wanted to

visualize my career as a whole wall, not just brick by brick. And the medium showed me a vision. I can remember it as if it were yesterday. She showed me a long low dilapidated tumble-down overgrown ruined wall. I was devastated. "Is this it? Is this my life?" She said: "Look along to the end of it." And I looked, and there, at the far end, beyond the collapsed hopes and ruined dreams, if I had the will to pick my way to it, was a slender gleaming pencil-thin turret, whose pinnacle touched the stars!

Regina And what did it signify, this erection?

Stella You can scoff Regina. It's this vision that's kept me going. It's why I've never been cast down by disappointments, and I've had plenty of them, haven't we all! It's just that I know, I've always known, that I have a destiny, and it's a cliché, but I will reach the stars. But not till the autumn of my career. Which is now.

Regina What are you planning? Banana skins on the stairs? Metal filings in the coffee?

Stella I don't know. It's uncanny. It's a premonition. I feel sick with knowing. That's why I'm on edge. It's nothing personal against Trixie. I love her. She's wonderful. But it's a dog-eats-dog world and she understands that better than anyone. She admits it in her book. She clawed her way to the top on the backs of her friends. She loved them, they were wonderful—

Regina But bitch eats bitch.

Tannoy Announcement Fifteen seconds to lights up on Act I Scene Three, thank you. (*Audience applause. Cuts out*)

Regina When I was just leaving the High Barnet Academy of Euphony and the Spoken Word, I went to see a bricklayer, and he showed me a brick wall and he said: "This is your life. Get used to beating your head against it."

Stella I've no sympathy if your only refuge is mockery.

Regina And knitting.

Stella What do you get out of it?

Regina Shawls, cardigans.

Stella What do you get out of twenty-five years as a clone between stairs that's never seen the light of the stage? Twenty-five years! Your Silver Jubilee! It happened, and no one noticed!

Regina The actual date isn't till a week on Wednesday.

Pause

Stella Let's have a party.

Regina Let's not.
Stella A special party. I'll talk to Charles. We'll invite everyone to stay behind after the show: the Dame, Trixie, P.Q. We'll *make* them come. We won't allow them to leave the theatre. Suddenly everyone will know that we exist! Now that's *chutzpah*.
Regina I thought you had to be Jewish to have *chutzpah*.
Stella I am Jewish. Slightly.
Regina And mad.
Stella I am mad. And frustrated, and pressured, and bored bored bored! God this stuffy little room! (*She throws herself on the chaise*) Don't you feel like Masha in *The Three Sisters*.
Regina Don't ask me to whistle. It's not the superstition, just that it carries.
Stella And we wouldn't want anyone knowing we were here would we—buried alive!
Regina It's the same with flushing the toilet. That's why there's a tradition of peeing in the sink.
Stella You are pathetic. You learn lines, you rehearse, you come in at the stage door on the half, you sit in the dressing-room, you read *The Stage*, you pee in the sink—
Regina How dare you accuse me of reading *The Stage*!
Stella Then when the show's over, you switch off the lights round your mirror and go out into the milling crowds, unnoticed, unrecognized, unfulfilled, because you haven't *acted*. You haven't done what you believe in, what you're trained and being paid for. You've done all the things that an actor does, except *act*. You've missed the experience, the essence, the roar of the greasepaint, the magic! Do you believe in magic?
Regina Nope.
Stella You don't?
Regina No.
Stella You can actually sit in a dressing-room and say you do not believe in the magic of the theatre?
Regina I believe the magic of the theatre is in the eye of the audience.
Stella What a desperately forlorn thing to say.
Regina All acting is sleight of hand.
Stella What about stage presence, star quality?
Regina I can knit one purl one, click click, clackety-clack, and turn a ball of wool into a jumper. I know how it's done.
Stella What's your purpose in life, Regina?

Act I, Scene 3

Regina To get to Sainsbury's tomorrow morning.

The Lights fade

SCENE 3

The dressing-room, next day, before the performance. Stella is doing lines with Charles

Stella/Helen Rejoice, rejoice! In Freedom's name rejoice!
Join hands ye wives in joy at tyrant slain!
My sister hath her husband's head split wide . . .

Regina enters, breathless, with carrier bags

Regina Sorry. Queue at the check-out. Then I missed the bus . . .
Stella/Helen —and with her righteous axe hath freed all wives!
Charles Trixie's looking fragile. We're doing lines.
Stella/Helen Rehearse again. How did this monster die?
Regina I heard her hawking and spitting as I came up. She sounded fine.
Stella/Helen —that I may savour well this sacred deed . . .
Charles It's just a winter snuffle, but she is seventy-five.
Stella/Helen How didst thou slay the dreadful despot? Say!
Regina/Clytemnestra I slew no despot but my dearest lord . . . (*She fills the kettle*)
Stella/Helen Say how he naked rose from his foul bath.
Regina Tea anyone?
Charles "Whose flesh . . ."
Regina/Clytemnestra (*unpacking*) Whose flesh had oft embrac'd my gentle flesh . . .
Stella/Helen How clefst thou his proud skull from crown to chin?
Regina Who's for some melon?
Charles I clove . . .
Regina/Clytemnestra I clove his gracious head with one fell blow—Kzzah! (*She cuts the melon karate-style*)
Tannoy Announcement Quarter of an hour please, ladies and gentlemen. This is your quarter of an hour call.

Regina/Clytemnestra (*eating the juicy melon*)
> And from his gushing crimson throat uprose
> a dreadful sigh: My love, why murder love?

Stella I want to do this on set.

Regina/Clytemnestra (*slurping*) Why dye these walls and water
> butcher red . . .?

Whoops sorry . . .

Stella Come on Regina. There's still time.

Charles It is after the quarter love.

Regina/Clytemnestra Why break the bond of home? Why curse our
> house?

Stella Charles will you go and find P.Q.? Tell him we're on stage rehearsing.

Charles He's not in tonight.

Stella (*desperately*) Why *not*?

Regina/Clytemnestra Our children why inflame their trusting eyes?

Stella Tonight of all nights! Ye gods! What are you doing to us?

Charles I did ask him, I did, if we could run you on set, and he just smiled, you know the way he does. (*He smiles*)

The kettle boils

Regina/Clytemnestra (*making tea*) Then through red steam I saw a
> sight more grim
> e'en than this kingly carcase. Gods forbear!
> I saw my son—

Stella What about my costume?

Regina/Clytemnestra   . . . eyes wide with hate, the seeds
> of vengeance sown . . .

Stella What do I *wear*?

Regina Do you want me to go on?

Stella I don't have a *costume*.

Charles Well we're hoping the situation might not arise—

Stella No we are not!

Charles Let's try and look on the bright side—

Stella This *is* the bright side Charles. I *want* to go on. It's my chance, my *duty*! And if a disaster is the only way of effecting that, well I'm sorry, that is what I have professionally undertaken. That is what undertaking is all about.

Regina Undertaking?

Stella We are a professional emergency service. Like the Fire Brigade.
Regina/Clytemnestra I swung the axe to slay my luckless son . . .
Stella It's been the same story all along.
Regina/Clytemnestra —then slay my coarse accursed loathsome self . . .
Stella Shut up Regina! We talked about it weeks ago. We were to have a run on stage at least once a week, and duplicate costumes—
Charles I don't think costumes are in the budget love.
Stella No but *we* are, or did someone forget we existed?
Regina You use hers.
Charles Reg knows.
Stella Who's hers?
Regina Trixie's.
Stella But she's wearing it, Regina.
Regina The moment she's down—
Charles Steady Reg love—
Regina . . . you haul her into the wings, strip the rags from her carcass—
Charles Let's keep calm, shall we, loves . . .
Stella I'm not going on. I'm sorry. I'm getting emotional. I shouldn't have to *think* about costumes. I'm doing *lines*!
Regina/Clytemnestra Blood blinded me—!
Stella My God, why is everyone so complacent?
Charles You could use your rehearsal skirt.
Stella It's black, Charles.
Charles They'll understand—
Stella Helen's costume is *red*. The rehearsal skirt is *black*. Are you asking the audience to understand there is no difference between *red* and *black*?
Regina/Clytemnestra Blood blinded me—!
Stella They're out there! They've paid money! They're waiting! They're on edge! They're expecting a *shock*—which I am contracted to provide, but not if I have to wander on like some dowdy, crumpled, under-rehearsed baglady!
Regina I thought that's what Helen was.
Charles I'll see what wardrobe's capable of coming up with, love.

Charles exits

Regina/Clytemnestra And in that moment did my son escape.

Stella/Helen He's gone. Grieve not for him.
Regina/Clytemnestra   By Heaven and Hell
  I swore then only till mother sheathe blade
  in flesh of son, or son his blade in mother—
Stella/Helen But thy son is dead. A messenger
  thou sayst did come this day to tell thee so.
Regina/Clytemnestra Not dead—
Stella/Helen   Aye so—
Regina/Clytemnestra   He lives—
Stella/Helen   No more—
Regina/Clytemnestra   I lied.
Stella/Helen A messenger from Phokis came t'announce
  Orestes thy grown son lies in his grave.
Regina/Clytemnestra He lies indeed. I lied to tell thee so.
Stella/Helen Then tell me true what truth lay in his lie?
Regina/Clytemnestra One summer's day, some score of years ago . . .
Stella Can we cut to my next speech please?
Regina/Clytemnestra . . . my two years' son was riding joyously on
  his father's galloping shoulders . . .
Stella Regina?
Regina/Clytemnestra   "Catch me Mamma"
  shouted he. "Come catch me if thou canst . . .!"
Stella May we do *my* lines?
Regina/Clytemnestra . . . I saw the bough and called—
Stella Please?
Regina/Clytemnestra   . . . Too late! It struck
  his tiny brow. He fell. I ran to him,
  and bore him to the bath and bathed his wound,
  and bound his broken head . . .
Stella So selfish . . .
Regina/Clytemnestra   . . . and kissed him, prayed:
  "God make thee well . . ."
Stella . . . utterly utterly selfish and self-indulgent . . .
Regina/Clytemnestra   And God the Healer healed
  my darling son leaving a whiten'd scar
  t'adorn his brow. That self-same scar adorn'd
  the brow of him that came from Phokis . . .

Pause

Act I, Scene 3

Charles enters with a red costume

Charles (*with a flourish*) Here we are then!
Regina She's in a sulk.
Charles What do you think of it?
Regina It's a bit garish.
Charles It might have to be broken down. It's Trixie's old costume from Act One, remember?
Regina She refused to wear it.
Charles She was so sweet about it, but it *was* too baggy and wrinkly in the hips.
Regina She said she wasn't going to go farting round the stage like a deflating balloon.
Charles (*to Stella*) Would you like to try it on love? Luckily you're not as slim as Trixie so it should fit . . .

Stella takes the costume in silence and goes behind the screen

(*To Regina*) Do you think she'll get into it?
Regina If she doesn't breathe.
Charles It was a stroke of luck, mixed with genius, I have to say it.
Regina You say it Charles. No one else will.
Charles I was sure it had been cannibalized into the costume for Act Three, but there it was on her rail.
Regina You took it from her room?
Charles She was doing her yoga, coughing horribly. She didn't see me.
Regina I bet she did.

Pause

Charles I shouldn't have taken it, I know, without authority.
Regina We'll blame you, Charles.
Charles P.Q. hates decisions being taken behind his back.
Regina Well you've done it now, haven't you? There's no going back. You really have done it now Charles . . .
Tannoy Announcement This is your five minute call. Five minutes please ladies and gentlemen.

Stella appears in a tight-fitting floor-length scarlet classical Greek dress

Stella How do I look?
Regina Like a tomato. Slightly boiled.

Charles You look fabulous.
Stella If I breathe in . . . and we make a couple of darts—
Charles Do you mean vents?
Regina She means rips. (*She rips two slits in the back of the dress*)
Stella Don't! You're ruining it!
Regina Is that better?
Stella You've destroyed it!
Regina You'd have ripped it yourself as soon as you tried moving.
Charles At least you can breathe now, love.
Stella Look at it. I shall look like a tramp.
Regina But you are a tramp. You've been tramping across Greece.
Charles You could cover the slits with the shawl.
Stella Shawl. I shall need a shawl. Where's my shawl?
Charles I don't think we have a spare shawl, love.
Regina You use Trixie's.
Charles Reg knows.
Stella I can't!
Regina You just take it.
Stella Have you seen the way she clutches it? It's in her character—her gnarled fingers like knots.
Regina Just break them. It's an emergency.
Stella (*an idea occurring*) There is a shawl I *could* use.
Regina It's not yours.
Stella But you were going to give it to me.
Regina But you don't like it.
Stella I *do* like it.
Regina You said you didn't.
Stella I was confused. You mustn't hold it against me.
Regina I won't hold it anywhere near you.
Charles Am I missing something here, loves?
Stella Regina is knitting me a shawl and it's just the thing. (*She holds it up*)
Charles No. No it's not right.
Regina And it's not finished.
Stella I'll take it as it is. (*She takes the needles out*)
Regina Don't take the needles out!
Stella I'm sorry Regina—
Regina It'll come to pieces.
Stella I've got to have a shawl! Something to clutch—it's in the character . . .

Act I, Scene 3   21

Charles It's the wrong colour. It's the wrong period.
Stella It hunches the shoulders, don't you think, makes me older, because remember I'm having to play older than I really am.
Charles It's utterly inappropriate.
Stella We can break it down if it's too new. (*She rumples it*)
Charles P.Q. would have a *fit*!
Stella It's unravelling . . . It's coming to pieces, Regina. Will you do something about it? (*She gives it to her*)
Regina (*bitterly*) Would you object very much if I stuck the needles back in?
Charles I think, Stella love, you may have to use Trixie's shawl.
Stella I'm not going to argue Charles. It's decided.
Charles P.Q. would insist on it.
Stella I'm using *my* shawl. As soon as it's ready Regina.
Charles Stella love . . .
Stella It's right because it makes me feel old, and at the same time, proud.
Charles You don't have to be so old. It was the one thing the critics said about Trixie. She was too old.
Stella Do you know how old Helen was?
Charles She was never as old as Trixie.
Stella Seventy-five.
Charles She wasn't!
Stella You can work it out. Because she and Clytemnestra . . .
Regina (*fixing the shawl*)—were quads with Castor and Pollux . . .
Stella —who couldn't have been less than fifteen, when they sailed with the Argonauts . . .
Regina —which was thirty-five years before the start of the Trojan War . . .
Stella —which puts Helen at fifty when she went . . .
Regina —and sixty when she came back . . .
Stella —and over *seventy*, and more probably seventy-*five* when finally, in the play, cast out by her wicked stepsons, she comes home to her sister in Argos (*emotionally*) destitute and begging for shelter . . .
Charles I didn't know you'd done all this research.
Regina Oh she's not just the fairest face in all the world.
Stella And do you know how old Paris was when they met?
Regina She's going to tell us.
Stella Seventeen.

Tannoy Announcement Beginners on stage please. Stand by beginners for Act One . . .

Charles You stay here, love. I'm just going check that Trixie's OK . . . (*He doesn't go*)

Stella And do you know how they met and became lovers all those years ago?

Regina (*yawning*) *Etonne-moi.*

Stella That night when the young prince came to the palace at Sparta, and the king was away in Crete . . . and the Queen in her kindness welcomed the boy and gave him apples and wine . . . and he was so dusty from his journey, she bathed him . . . and he was so tired . . .

Fade to Black-out

Scene 4

A performance is in progress. The voice of Trixie is heard over the main speakers

Trixie/Helen   . . . Smiling he told me
       how he grew in strength and proved his princeship
       to the King his father, who bedazzl'd
       by the burning eyes, reclaim'd his son,
       unmindful of the danger—as was I,
       who now did let him laughing raise my hand
       and close his fiery lips upon my rings.
       Those wedding bands that bound me to my lord
       he loosed with spittle, turned with tongue and teeth
       and drew them to my quiv'ring finger-ends . . .

Her voice fades

Lights up on the dressing-room. Stella, costumed, is in front of her mirror, completing her make-up: white face, black eyes, red lips. Regina knits, finishing the shawl. Charles is reading on the couch

Stella It's like drowning. The whole of one's life passes in front of one.

Regina Do you want to play memory games?

Act I, Scene 4

Stella One's first love . . . in the moonlight . . . That song, if I can remember it . . .
Regina "Unforgettable"?
Stella (*singing*) "Roses are shining in Picardy . . ."
Regina That's going back a bit.
Stella He was shell-shocked. He told me how they'd set off, volunteers, only seventeen some of them, singing away like heroes! Then in a few days, they were in the trenches, waiting, sick with fear, for the signal to go over the top . . .
Regina Was this the *First* World War?
Stella I was so young.
Regina You weren't born.
Stella He was telling me this in whispers, as I lay in his arms, years later, in a Shropshire cornfield.
Regina Shropshire's nice.
Stella Then suddenly, without warning, just as the shells were beginning to explode again in his mind, he cried out and smothered me with his face, his whole body tense and shaking with spasms, unable to bear the memory.
Regina I don't think that was shell-shock Stella.
Stella It was my first experience of Theatre. The magic that rules life. (*Pause*) We had a child. I don't know how anyone who has never had a child can call herself an actress. Have you ever had a child, Regina?
Regina Nope.
Stella Of course I couldn't keep him. I'd taken a conscious decision to put career before happiness.
Regina I'd taken a conscious decision not to take conscious decisions.
Stella Where is he now I wonder? He'd be about your age Charles.
Charles (*in his book*) What?
Regina She's your mother.
Stella (*looking in the mirror*) These lips aren't right. How does Trixie do it? Does she have lips?
Regina She lost them in the last face-lift.
Stella Cupid's bow or crimson gash? I want advice, Regina.
Regina Go for the gash.
Stella But Clytemnestra would say that wouldn't she? Helen I feel is more . . . labially manipulative. She leads with her lips. She was ravished when she was nine, by Theseus. Did you know that? It

taught her to be exceptionally careful with older men. Did you know she ruled the whole of Greece virtually single-handed, through having all the old kings eating out of her hand because she would not decide whom to marry. I so understand her. I am her. She is me . . .

Regina has finished the shawl. She places it on Stella's shoulders

Regina Here's your shawl.
Stella Oh . . .
Regina Break a leg.
Stella (*overcome*) Regina . . .!
Regina Don't kiss me. You'll spoil your lips.
Stella I'm going to cry.
Regina You'll spoil your eyes.
Stella It's so soft, so alive . . .! You *do* like it, Charles.
Charles (*reading*) What?
Stella And don't say it's out of period. It can't be. It's so natural. It's wool.
Regina It's not actually.
Stella It's not man-made. It can't be.
Charles I'm sorry love. It's not on.
Stella Isn't it divine?
Regina It's not man-made.
Stella I knew it wasn't.
Regina It's goat.
Stella What?
Regina Goat.
Charles I just know P.Q. will go berserk—!
Stella What do you mean *goat*? Goats don't *have* wool.
Regina It's hair.
Stella *Hair?*
Regina The hair of the Angora goat.
Stella (*hunching her shoulders*) Suddenly I'm beginning to be a little less fond of it.
Charles I'm sure you could use Trixie's.
Stella It's making me tense, constricting the shoulders, making them angular, like a bird's . . .
Regina Do birds have shoulders?
Stella Like the poisoned wedding-dress in *Medea* which could never be removed, which turned the bride into a hag . . .

Act I, Scene 5

Regina It killed her actually.
Stella Regina!
Regina But that was not my intention Stella, honestly.
Stella (*wrestling with it*) It won't come off! I'm burning!
Regina It was just a gift, dear.
Charles Stella—
Regina Let her sizzle a bit.
Stella I'm shrinking! I'm *ageing*! Oh Regina, you've done it! I'm old . . .!
Regina Who wants to play memory games?
Stella Seventy-five! I am *old* and *proud* to be old . . . I feel . . . I know . . . I *am* Helen . . . AaaAAaah . . . (*A low tragic moan*)
Regina I went to Sainsbury's and in my trolley I put an apple.
Charles I went to Sainsbury's and in my trolley I put an apple and a banana.
Regina I went to Sainsbury's and in my trolley I put an apple, a banana, and a carrot . . .

Fade to Black-out

Scene 5

The dressing-room. Later. Stella is sitting aged and dignified in the constricting shawl. Regina is knitting another one. Charles has gone

Stella I went to Sotheby's and in my transit-van I put . . . an altarpiece, a Baroque sideboard, a Caravaggio, a diamond tiara . . .
Regina You're superstitious aren't you, Stella?
Stella Not especially . . . an Elgin marble, a Fabergé egg . . . I wouldn't whistle in the dressing-room or quote the Scottish play—
Regina I'm wearing green stockings.
Stella Oh, heavens, that doesn't bother me.
Regina It didn't occur to me. I'm terribly sorry.
Stella I don't regard that as unlucky.
Regina But if you believe in magic—
Stella Don't go on about it, Regina. A Gutenburg Bible . . .
Regina But if you believe in magic, as you do, you must worry about—

Stella The only thing I worry about is keeping calm for my performance . . .
Regina I thought you liked to be on edge.
Stella And Helen.
Regina Helen?
Stella Helen of Troy. A Gutenburg Bible and Helen of Troy.
Regina But you're Helen of Troy.
Stella Are you challenging?
Regina And she's not inanimate. She'd never go in your transit van.
Stella I don't want to play this any more. (*She turns up the tannoy*)
Trixie/Helen (*over the tannoy—defying her state of health*)
        Alone, thy lord at Troy, lov'dst thou no man.
        Thy lonely bed did no well-favour'd knight . . .
Regina It's nearly the interval.
Trixie/Helen —no equerry, no beau, gallant or swain,
        no stable lad or brawny butcher boy . . .
Stella She's not going to make it.
Trixie/Helen —slip slyly in? Didst yield to no man's wiles?
Regina Thank God for the Dame.
Dame/Clytemnestra I yielded to Aegisthus, not in love . . .
Regina She's a rock.
Stella She acts like one.

Regina mimes to the Dame

Dame/Clytemnestra One stark, storm-blacken'd night he came to me . . .
        brought down his bulk upon me; I did yield . . .
Stella I cannot believe this performance.
Dame/Clytemnestra Coarse callus'd were those hands that scrap'd and scour'd
        my skin; his breath, foul gaseous exhalations
        in my face . . .
Stella Yeugh! I can't listen. (*She turns the tannoy down*)
Dame/Clytemnestra (*fading*)—as fat and rank his barb'rous
        pock-mark'd flesh crush'd me . . .
Stella She hasn't suffered. No life experience. She hasn't lived. Was she ever married?
Regina She murdered her husband.

Stella She didn't!
Regina No, she didn't.
Stella Has she had children?
Regina I don't know.
Stella You don't know?
Regina I don't know her.
Stella But you've understudied her for twenty-five years.
Regina I only know her professionally.
Stella And you've never wanted to find out?
Regina She trusts me not to be interested.
Stella Hasn't she ever, in a rash moment, spoken to you?
Regina She ignores me. That's the basis of our relationship.
Stella What a tragically missed opportunity!
Regina It's like a marriage. I walk beside her wherever she goes and she pretends I'm not there. Like a shop window. I'm her reflection for her to check herself against.
Stella I'd have thought after all this time you'd be a sort of confidante. Like a dresser, but without the nuisance of laundry.
Regina I am her storage. I store her performance. I know it better than she does, because I don't have to do it, just keep it. I even know when she breathes. I am her librarian. I've got all her performances intact, play by play. I am her archive, and being a rock of the theatre, the one "constant star", she is absolutely dependent on me. Haven't you seen her sometimes creeping in when we're rehearsing, like the cleaning lady?
Stella That *was* the cleaning lady.
Regina She fears me. I am the slave in the chariot of the triumphal general who whispers in his ear: Remember you are mortal . . . Remember you are mortal . . . Remember you are mortal . . .
Stella Not much of a part.
Regina I am her conscience, her insurance. She can't go on without me, and she cannot be off if I'm there. And she has never has been, not once in twenty-five years,—no that's wrong, now I remember, there was one occasion, when I wasn't there, and she was in Leeds playing Lady Macbeth—
Stella (*choking*) Ach.

Pause

Regina Oh. Sorry.
Stella (*as if poisoned*) Aaaaach . . .

Regina What do I do? Go out, turn round three times, stand on my head . . .?

Stella There's . . . no . . . antidote . . .

Regina Anyway, as I was saying, I was away. I'd got the night off to go to a concert which my nephew was in. He's a bassoonist, quite talented—

Stella Tonight of all nights. You did it on purpose! You're evil!

Regina And she was on as Lady M, it was the sleep-walking scene and she came on and she said—

Stella Don't say it—

Regina She said—

Stella (*blocking her ears*) No! No!

Regina She didn't say anything. She dried stone dead. Which was fortunate.

Stella I hate you. I curse you. I curse your *shawl*! Poisoned goat's hair! Eeeurgh . . . (*She tears it off*)

Regina I'll take it back then; give it to someone who'll appreciate the labour, the expense . . .

Stella You've robbed the theatre of its magic, reduced it to sleight of hand, memory games—!

Regina (*folding the shawl and putting it neatly under her cushion*) I went to Dunsinane—

Stella *No!*

Regina And in my cauldron I sloshed—

Stella Shut up! Shut up! No! No . . .! (*She continues*)

Regina . . . an adder, a blindworm, sow's blood, liver of blaspheming Jew, nose of Turk and Tartar's lips, grease that's sweaten from the murderer's gibbet . . .

Tannoy Announcement (*urgently*) Miss Widgery to the prompt corner immediately please.

Silence

Miss Widgery *at once* to the prompt corner . . .

Regina Stella, that's you.

Pause

Charles bursts into the room

Charles Stella, you're on! Trixie's fainted. Weren't you listening? They've brought the curtain down. They're waiting . . .

Act I, Scene 5

Pause

Tannoy (*Desperately*) Miss Widgery will you come to the corner *now*?
Charles Stella . . . this is your chance . . .

Stella rises

Stella Thank you Charles . . .
Tannoy *Stella Widgery where are you?*
Charles She's coming . . .
Stella Step aside please.

Stella makes her exit

Charles Truly she is no longer an understudy. She is a star . . .
Regina Pardon me while I impale myself.

Pause. They wait to hear her over the tannoy

Stella bursts back in

Stella The shawl! The shawl! I don't have the *shawl*!
Charles It's in the wings love. Use Trixie's.
Stella (*searching frantically*) I must have it! Where is it? Regina where is it? The *shawl*!
Charles You don't need the shawl!
Stella (*distractedly*) I was all ready and waiting, all prepared. I had everything *ready*!
Charles Go on, Stella love. It's your moment. You're missing it.
Stella (*still looking*) Regina you took it. Where is it? Where did you put it?

Applause is heard over the tannoy as the action restarts

I'm not going on without it. I can't. It's the character. I know it's silly but it's the way it hunches the shoulders, because remember I'm having to play older than I really am . . .

The Dame and Trixie are again heard over the tannoy

Trixie/Helen Forgive me sister, I am old and tired.
Stella It makes me old you see . . . old . . .
Dame/Clytemnestra I never shall forgive what thou hast done.
Regina (*finding the shawl*) Oh, here it is. I was sitting on it. (*She puts it round Stella's shoulders*)
Trixie/Helen Oh hold me, raise me, house me, I implore . . .

Stella (*huddling into the shawl*) . . . old . . . and tired . . .
Charles It's all right now, love.
Dame/Clytemnestra I never shall forget thy poisonous ways . . .
Charles Trixie's back now. Panic over.
Stella (*shivering, sobbing*) . . . old . . . old . . .
Trixie/Helen I love thee sister, love me I implore . . .
Charles It'll be the interval in a moment. She'll be all right now . . . All right . . .?
Trixie/Helen My lord is dead and by his sons I am
    cast out. Oh sister, on my knees I cry.
    Curse not your own, but raise me in thine arms
    that we in age may heal youth's ancient wounds . . .

       CURTAIN

ACT II

Scene 1

The dressing-room. P.Q. seated comfortably. He is young-looking, in black leather, with sculpted beard. Amiable and dangerous. Charles, awkward, is waiting

Charles I can't think what's happened to them. I did call them. I'm sure I called them, though I didn't of course warn them you were coming, P.Q. They wouldn't *need* warning. They're so professional. Last night when you weren't in, I don't know what you've heard, but they were marvellous. When Trixie collapsed, they were quietly, almost unnoticeably, *marvellous.* They sensed Trixie wasn't well and you should have seen them, as it were, shifting almost imperceptibly into gear, so that when the moment came and Stella was called, she was absolutely ready, she really was, word perfect, like a greyhound in the slips.

P.Q. stirs

I did tell them, I'm sure I told them. I can't think where they've got to! They're normally so absolutely on time, you wouldn't notice. They're living proof—if proof is necessary—that they're *necessary,* I mean they belong, as part of the fabric, because one can so easily dismiss, I mean disregard the understudy, but that's like overlooking the underlay, which you don't see but you'd notice if it wasn't there. You'd notice the insecurity.

P.Q. unzips his jacket, takes out his pocket phone, and smiles

I mean you'd have noticed them last night, you really would, if they hadn't been there . . . I mean if you'd been there . . . and they hadn't been . . . I don't believe they're not here . . .

Charles goes to find them

P.Q. punches a number

P.Q. Darling it's P. It's about Trixie. Keep this under wraps but she may croak . . . By all the laws of angina and lung disease she should be dead as a doornail, though being Trixie of course she doesn't agree, and I cherish her, I swear by her I do, from her first cigarette to her last dying gin. She's immortal. However, unfortunately, immortality is not enough. If Trixie is looking wobbly, she must be underpinned. And I mean bankably. We need a name my darling, just to cover for the duration . . . No, listen to me, sweetheart. Someone known, a Known Actress . . . (*He continues confidentially*)

Regina, Stella and Charles come in

Stella (*crossing herself*) Angels and ministers of grace defend us . . .
Regina I'm going to murder you for this, Charles.
Charles (*hurrying them behind the screen to change*) But it's what you wanted loves. You don't know what it took to persuade . . .
Stella It's a betrayal of our trust . . .
Regina It's the end of needlework as we know it . . .

They change behind the screen

P.Q. (*on the phone*) Super. Get her to call me on the mobile . . . You can promise her she will have all the frills and fairy-dust of the superstar! (*Confidentially*) She will even have her own understudy . . . (*He rings off, smiles and settles back*)
Charles (*emerging*) They'll be with us in just a second P.Q. They were in the green room! Total miscommunication. My fault entirely! (*Calling*) Are you ready yet girls? Time is money . . .

Pause. Charles sits, opens the book. They wait

Regina and Stella appear from either side of the screen in black skirts and shawls, their hair tied back. They position themselves

Charles (*to P.Q.*) No flesh . . .? (*To Regina and Stella*) No flesh . . .
Stella/Helen No flesh has touched thy flesh for ten years?
Regina/Clytemnestra None.
Stella/Helen No mortal hand caressed thy cheek?
Regina/Clytemnestra Not one.
Stella/Helen No long'd-for whisper'd comfort?
Regina/Clytemnestra Not one word.
P.Q. (*to Charles*) Who's Clytemnestra?

Act II, Scene 1

Charles Regina.
Stella/Helen Then shall I break the spell—
Regina/Clytemnestra   Dare not come near—!
P.Q. What the fuck are you doing, Regina?
Charles But she prefers Reg. She prefers you to call her Reg.
P.Q. You're spouting like a fucking tea-pot. What are you spouting like?
Charles (*consulting the book*) Doesn't the Dame use that gesture?
P.Q. You've got to stop her, sweetheart, or she'll touch you. This is Helen. She's in a touching mood, aren't you Helen?
Stella Oh yes!
P.Q. And her touch is a thousand volts. She'll light you up!
Stella/Helen Then shall I . . . light you up—!
Regina/Clytemnestra   Dare not come near—!
P.Q. Did you *train* as a traffic warden?
Regina No.
P.Q. What the fuck are you then?
Regina I am an understudy.
P.Q. You're the Queen . . . (*Pause*) Not our own dear Queen who quite possibly *did* train as a traffic warden.

Stella laughs

    You are the Queen of Angus, the Axe Murderess! This is the day of your death. You are ascending the steps to the Temple . . .
Charles I think that's the problem, P.Q. . . .
P.Q. And this electromagnetic rabid pariah-bitch is going to stop you.
Charles We don't have the steps . . .
P.Q. How the fuck are you going to get past her?
Regina In the same way as the Dame gets past . . .

Pause

Stella Sorry P.Q., but *I* don't see myself as a "rabid bitch" do I . . .? *I* don't have that conception . . .?
P.Q. (*suddenly angry*) Your jobs are on the line! You are about to be sacked! There is no security in this profession! We do not carry passengers!
Regina/Clytemnestra (*equally angry*) Dare! Not! Come! Near—!
P.Q. Try threatening. Lower the voice.
Charles But the Dame doesn't do that.

P.Q. (*quietly*) Lower the voice.
Regina/Clytemnestra   (*quitely*) Dare not come near. Since Agamemnon's death, no flesh, no hand, no word of comfort hath infected me . . .
P.Q. Go on.
Charles (*shaking his head*) It's not correct . . .
Stella/Helen Oh how thy life is wasted!
Regina/Clytemnestra   I have killed.
Stella/Helen Would *I* had kill'd my lord as thou kill'dst thine! Would *I* had splinter'd his proud head . . . (*Dries*) Yes . . .?
Charles (*prompting*) I'd cry . . .
Stella/Helen I'd cry . . .
P.Q. Go on.
Charles Freedom . . .
P.Q. Improvise.
Stella/Helen Improvise! Be free! Tear yourselves free from the bonds of fate . . .! I've forgotten the lines . . . Just *live*! Break the chains! It's *life* that matters—*your* life! Make something *of* it! Don't let *any* soldier-husband come home from the wars, and kennel you in, like a bitch on heat—!
P.Q. Yes, yes . . .!

P.Q.'s phone rings

Stella You are the Queen!
P.Q. (*on the phone*) Yes, yes . . .
Stella The Queen of your *life* . . .!
P.Q. (*on the phone*) Darling, you'll have to speak up . . .
Stella Speak up . . .? (*Louder*) *Vivat Regina*! Celebrate! Celebrate your Jubilee . . .!
P.Q. (*on the phone*) Sweetheart you sound desperate . . .
Stella Desperate . . .? (*Desperately*) Unfurl the banners! Follow your star! Go for broke! Be free . . .!
P.Q. (*out of hearing—on the phone*) Are you willing to cover Trixie . . .
Charles (*prompting*) But I was made . . .
Stella/Helen But I was made of less stern stuff than thou . . .
P.Q. (*on the phone*) I didn't say "understudy" my sweet, I said "cover" . . .
Charles I lured . . .

Act II, Scene 2   35

Stella/Helen I lur'd appeal'd deceiv'd, but thou didst kill . . .
P.Q. (*on the phone*) Marvellous! Let's go for it . . .
Stella/Helen (*going for it*) Be proud, be known! Thy deed all mine outshines!
P.Q. (*on the phone*) Tea and scones. Now. The Savoy. (*He rings off*)
Regina/Clytemnestra My son awaits within yon temple door—
P.Q. (*getting up*) Sorry Charles. No rest for the wicked. Darlings you're marvellous. Especially last night. Regina. (*He puts his arm round her*) Charles says you were marvellous.
Regina It was Stella actually.
P.Q. Stella. (*He holds both her hands*) You were marvellous. (*He cuffs Charles*) Carry on, Charles. Don't stop for me . . .

P.Q. exits

The rehearsal continues

Regina/Clytemnestra My son awaits within yon temple door,
          and call'd to his supposed obsequies,
          I climb this stair; for shall I mortal know
          no mortal touch till my son's vengeful lips
          touch mine, and murd'ring steel invade this ancient
          murderer's breast . . .

Fade to Black-out

Scene 2

A matinee is in progress. Voices are heard over the main speakers

Trixie/Helen Thy son must be the age my Paris was.
Dame/Clytemnestra He's older, angrier, by more blows inflam'd.
Trixie/Helen Yet he must nurse the same desires of youth.
Dame/Clytemnestra Revenge is all he seeks, revenge on me.
Trixie/Helen I know the ways and dreams of boys like him.
Dame/Clytemnestra My life is his to crush by natural law.
Trixie/Helen But I could save thy life by sweetening his.
Dame/Clytemnestra What I did damns me. I must pay the price.

Trixie/Helen I'll pay. Old as I am, I am the life
that quick'ns the loins of boys till they do spurt
their jets of seed like surging foam . . .

Their voices fade

Lights come up on the dressing-room. Regina is knitting, Stella is on edge

Stella Why did he have to rush out?
Regina He couldn't contain himself.
Stella What did he think of us really?
Regina We were marvellous.
Stella No, really. Do you think he enjoyed it?
Regina P.Q. always enjoys it.
Stella *I* enjoyed it. I was good.
Regina What do you mean by "good"?
Stella Inspired.
Regina Understudies aren't meant to be inspired. Or even good.
Stella What are they meant to be?
Regina OK. Just OK.
Stella Was I OK?
Regina You were good.

Pause

Stella How much do you think he really knows . . . about last night?
Regina It'll be in the stage management reports.
Stella What will?
Regina That Trixie fainted.
Stella And that I was absolutely ready to go on but couldn't find my shawl. Will he hold that against me?
Regina He's already said you were marvellous.
Stella You mean for insisting on not going on till I was absolutely ready?
Regina For not going on. He doesn't like understudies.
Stella I agree with him. They're a motley mealy-mouthed self-effacing little crew—present company excepted!
Regina Oh don't mind me.
Stella I've only done it once before, and I swore never again. Most dreadful experience. I won't name names but she said to me after seeing me in rehearsal, she said: "Stella, you will never go on for

Act II, Scene 2

me. I'd kill the show sooner than surrender my career into your hands!" I said "Why?" She said spitting: "Because you're *better* than me! Did you think I would allow my own shadow to eclipse me?"

Regina They can be so sarcastic.

Stella If I ever do go on, the audience will see Stella Widgery as Helen. I shall open my mouth and allow Helen to speak, (*she laughs*) and just hope she remembers her lines!

Regina If you ever do go on all the audience will do is hate you for not being what they paid for.

Stella Do you think he minded—when I . . . dried?

Regina He walked out.

Stella That was afterwards, after he'd said "Yes, yes!" when I was improvising. He *asked* me to improvise.

Regina He was saying "Yes yes" to the phone.

Stella No no—

Regina Yes yes. Then he walked out.

Stella After he'd told us we were marvellous.

Regina After he'd told us we were going to be sacked.

Stella He was just winding us up.

Regina Prior to letting us go.

Stella I didn't believe that for a moment!

Regina *I* didn't believe it, for a moment.

Pause

> (*As Clytemnestra*) My son will e'en disdain to laugh at thee.
> Thy shrunken painted lips, thy cak'd facade
> will launch no lusty foaming ship for him.
> He'll pale, screw up his eyes and turn away.

Do you have an agent?

Stella Why?

Regina Just asking.

Stella No. I did have, but we fell out. It was stupid. He said I had to change my name.

Regina Why didn't you?

Stella I did.

Regina You changed your name . . . to Stella Widgery?

Stella Yes.

Regina Have you had much work?
Stella (*sighing, then shrugging*) He *made* me change it, then the bastard said he couldn't market me after all. I said "I don't want to be marketed! I'm not a detergent!"
Regina What was your real name?
Stella I'm not telling you that!
Regina Oh go on.
Stella You'll laugh.
Regina I'll try not to.
Stella Phoebe. (*She giggles*)

Pause

Regina I like it.
Stella Oh stop—
Regina It suits you.
Stella It does not.
Regina It's a gentle, friendly, relaxing sort of name.
Stella It's a flimsy, mimsy, moony sort of name.
Regina It's you all over.
Stella I pity you Regina. I really pity you.
Regina Have you had lunch? (*She sets out her picnic from her bag*)
Stella You have no self-pride. P.Q. was really trying with you. He saw something *in* you, he truly did.
Regina Crisp?
Stella He *concentrated* on you. It was *you* he wanted to find out about. That's why he went for you, but you were just offended. You didn't rise to his challenge. So he just left. He was *with* us. He was *directing* us, but you wouldn't rise to him. So he gave up, and just left.
Regina Egg?
Stella It was so sad. You could be a great actress Regina . . .
Regina Given a nice meaty role to get my teeth into.
Stella Cleopatra, Lady Bracknell . . .
Regina (*eating a roll*) Tuna and coleslaw actually.
Stella You're in your prime. But you won't *see* it—that's the tragedy. You have such a talent but you will hide it under this silly, sarcastic *bushel*. No wonder you're embarrassed by your Jubilee. Twenty-five years of what? Nothing! Let's *not* celebrate then! Let's have a *non*-party. We'll invite no one and no one will come!

Act II, Scene 2

Pause

I'm sorry.
Regina Don't apologize.
Stella No, it was cruel.
Regina It was ironic. A bit heavy-handed, but you're learning.
Stella We've got to get out of this prison, both of us.
Regina We'll be out soon enough.
Tannoy Announcement Stand by for lights down on Act Two Scene Two . . .
Regina There's hardly anyone in this afternoon. They should cancel the matinees.
Stella (*with her eyes closed*) I can feel it coming . . . in spite of everything . . . something terrible, something wonderful, a kind of destiny . . .
Regina Oh dear.
Tannoy Announcement Ten seconds to lights up on Act Two Scene Three, thank you . . .
Stella I can see the stars, the whole panoply of the universe . . . But the difference is I now know this is a *shared* destiny Regina. If God willing I do make it onto the pedestal, I want you to be on it as well.
Regina Will there be room?
Stella Oh yes. There has to be! Or we could have one each.
Regina And what will we do on our bollards? Direct the traffic?
Stella (*laughing*) Don't be stupid!

Charles looks in

Charles Stella, my love . . .
Regina (*gesturing*) "Dare not come near!"

They laugh

Charles Stella, it's P.Q. He wants to see you.

Black-out

Scene 3

The same, later. Regina is knitting. Stella comes in

Regina Well? What did he say?
Stella Oh he was very nice. Quite sweet.
Regina Sweet?
Stella He took time to explain the situation from the director's point of view.
Regina While you minded your ps and qs.
Stella He just wouldn't stop smiling.
Regina How alarming.
Stella He told me, in confidence, that Trixie was under doctor's orders not to perform, but being Trixie she wouldn't hear of it, and any day now she was likely to be taken seriously ill, and might be off for several weeks.
Regina Then what?
Stella He said that as director he had to take stock . . .
Regina "Oh villain villain, smiling damned villain . . ."
Stella *(choking)* Ach.
Regina *Hamlet* . . . So he was just checking how to spell your name for the lights.
Stella Please don't be sarcastic, Regina.
Regina So he was just telling you your performance was so *awful* you couldn't be trusted—

Stella bursts into tears

Oh.
Stella *(sobbing)* He said I was good. He said my performance was really strong. I had a presence on stage, and it was quite clear I could handle a major part, and if he wasn't being "held over a barrel" by the box office—
Regina He's replacing you.
Stella I'm not known! I'm not a "known actress". He is going to have to engage someone who is "known to the public". So from tomorrow, until Trixie is completely better again, he said he's bringing in a Known Actress.
Regina Who is she?
Stella I'd never heard of her.

Regina I hope you said you'd agree to nothing till you'd spoken to your agent.
Stella I don't *have* an agent.
Regina But you did stand up to him.
Stella How could I? He as good as told me I didn't have a leg to stand up to him *on*.
Regina You're under contract as an understudy.
Stella I know and he said I was free to stay on as the understudy's understudy. He even made a joke of it.
Regina Oh that's all right then. For a moment I thought you were serious.
Stella I wish you'd stop making fun of me!
Regina (*attending to her knitting*) I wish you'd stop making fun of yourself. You'll have me in stitches. Four, eight, twelve, sixteen . . .
Stella You won't allow anyone to be serious.
Regina Do you want me to be serious?
Stella It would make a change.

Pause

Regina Go and sit in the audience.
Stella What?
Regina If you really believe understudies become stars overnight as in *Broadway Melody*, you belong in the audience.

Pause. Regina knits

Stella All right.
Regina You're too theatrical to be an actress. It's a technique. Like make-up.

Stella starts taking out sticks of make-up and throwing them at Regina

Stella All right, take it. Take it . . .

Regina continues knitting while being pelted

Regina It's about control.
Stella Take the bloody make-up . . . It's yours, all yours . . .
Regina Keeping a hold of yourself . . .
Stella Take all of it . . . Take the lot . . .
Regina Keeping something in reserve . . .
Stella Crimson lake! Nose putty! Kensington Gore . . .!
Regina Not going over the top, Stella.

Stella (*emptying a tin of powder over Regina*) Whores and clowns! Whores and clowns!
Regina Faking it, pretending . . .
Stella That's what my father said when I went into the business—
Regina It's just a game Stella.
Stella And he was right! I've wasted my life with whores and clowns!
Regina It's not real. It's "pretend" . . .
Stella (*hysterically hurling everything*) Take it! Take it! Take the whole whoring clowning paraphernalia—!

Stella hurls the make-up box which catches Regina a glancing blow on the temple. Regina goes flying over the back of her chair. Pause

Regina . . .? Reg . . .? Oh my God . . . I've killed her . . .

Silence

Regina (*in a low growl from behind the chair*) You bastard . . .
Stella Sorry, Reg . . .
Regina You've ruined it . . .
Stella No . . .
Regina (*emerging, her face streaming blood*) You've ruined my knitting . . .
Stella Help . . .
Regina I'm going to skewer you for this . . .
Stella (*struggling*) No, please . . .
Regina (*approaching with the knitting needle like a dagger*) I'm going to plunge this needle into your heart you little *worm*! You've upset me!
Stella Charles . . .?
Regina Didn't they tell you it's *dangerous* to upset an understudy?
Stella No . . . I didn't know . . .
Regina We're like time-bombs . . .
Stella (*writhing*) Aaah . . .
Regina —which have to be kept stable so they don't go off . . .
Stella (*grunting, struggling*) Oh please don't . . .
Regina And I was ticking away so nicely till you came along Stella. There was a pattern to my life. I was clicking away quite placidly, row by row, till you came in Stella. I was composed. I was unruffled. I was serene. But now I'm *snagged* . . . (*She chokes, breaks down*) unravelling . . . coming to pieces . . .
Stella Oh, Reg . . . I'm sorry . . .

Act II, Scene 3

Regina howls like an animal

Oh, what have I done . . .? Oh poor Reg . . .
Regina I'm all right. Don't touch me. I'm fine . . . (*She recovers completely*) Just pretending.
Stella You—
Regina Just acting. Technique. You should study it.
Stella (*wanting something to throw*) You *wretch* . . .
Regina Don't! It's not worth the blood. We only have one bottle. (*She begins to clean her face*)
Stella You monster . . .
Regina Look at this knitting.
Stella You clown . . .
Regina Have to start again. You can do it for me.
Stella I can't knit.
Regina I'll teach you. What do you want to make?

They sit together

Stella Oh, I don't know. A gown?
Regina Let's make a dish-cloth. (*She demonstrates*) Are you watching? This is casting on . . .
Stella Casting . . .?
Regina Make a loop, go through, go over, and out. Make a loop, and through, and pass it over, and out . . . Just think we don't have to worry about going on ever again.
Stella You do.
Regina It never worried me. Now you do it. (*She gives her the knitting*)
Stella Make a loop . . .? Go through . . .? Over and . . . out . . .
Regina No, no . . . (*She shows her*)
Stella Make a loop, go through, go over . . .
Regina And out . . . That's right . . .
Stella I expect she'll want extra rehearsals.
Regina Who will?
Stella The K.A.
Regina The who?
Stella The Known Actress.

Charles knocks, pops his head in

Charles Loves, there's an extra rehearsal tomorrow morning, ten o'clock, OK?

Charles goes

Stella Make a loop, go through, and over and out . . . Make a loop, go through and over and out . . . Make a loop, go through, and over and out . . .

The Lights fade

SCENE 4

Voices over the main speakers

Trixie/Helen My heart cries out!
Dame/Clytemnestra Thy heart's a Siren. I'll not heed its cry!
Trixie/Helen My once lithe limbs are strick'n!
Dame/Clytemnestra Full justly stricken are those limbs that once did coil like pois'nous snakes!
Trixie/Helen My soul wants peace!
Dame/Clytemnestra No peace be thine even in death—
Trixie/Helen Wouldst kill me?
Dame/Clytemnestra Yea, with these bare hands!
Trixie/Helen Come then bare hands—
Dame/Clytemnestra If I were sure thou'dst gain no peace—
Trixie/Helen Embrace—!
Dame/Clytemnestra I'd strangle thee—!

The voices fade

Lights come up on the dressing-room. The Known Actress, as Helen, is CS in red rehearsal skirt, red pumps, her red hair swept back. She has a script. Regina as Clytemnestra is in black. Charles is seated with the book. Stella sits quietly in a corner learning to knit

Known Actress/Helen Come strangle stifle choke, stop up this mouth and see if thou canst snuff th'eternal flame of life that was Jove's gift to men through his most dear adored daughter—(*As herself*) Woof! Where do you *breathe*? (*To Stella*) What was your name dear?

Stella My name is Stella.
Known Actress I'm going to be relying on you totally, Stella darling—such a pretty name. I'm so glad you're here. You won't leave me, darling.
Charles The breaths should be marked in the book but Trixie does vary.
Known Actress And *I* shall vary I promise you! (*To Regina*) What was your name, dear?
Regina Reg.
Known Actress Reg, I know it's not Christmas but you *are* going to have to give me something dear, not just stand about like a pudding! Cue?
Charles Strangle?
Regina } (*together*) I'll strangle . . .
Known Actress } Come strangle . . .
Known Actress (*laughing*) Could we please establish who's strangling whom? (*To Stella*) Darling you look so forlorn. Do try to cheer up.
Charles Your line, Reg.
Known Actress Wait a minute. Am I strangling you or are you strangling me?
Regina I'm not strangling—
Known Actress But you are going *into* a strangle, which I am embracing, unless I've got it totally wrong!
Regina The Dame doesn't strangle—
Known Actress Darling I'll only say this once. I don't want to know what the Dame does, or what Trixie does. *I* am doing what *I* am doing. It's in my contract.
Regina We don't touch.
Known Actress *I* touch. I am a tactile performer. Please accommodate me I beg you—what was your name, "Retch"?
Regina Reg.
Charles Short for Regina—
Known Actress I am old and tired and tactile, Retch—*burdened* by exile and a lifetime of divinity. (*To Stella*) I *am* divine aren't I, Stella darling? You've done the research. I'm not just putting it on.
Stella You're divine.
Known Actress Isn't she wonderful? I love knitting! (*To Regina*) You don't knit do you dear?
Regina Yes.

Known Actress I can tell you see. It's in the hands. (*She feels Regina's hands*) These knots . . . these poor hands. You should knit you know dear, then they won't—
Regina Get knotted.
Known Actress You're afraid of being touched aren't you?
Charles You don't in fact touch till . . . page ninety-three.
Known Actress Is that carved in stone?
Charles It's in the book.
Known Actress What was your name dear?
Charles Charles.
Known Actress Charles, I'm not going to say it twice, and it's no reflection I assure you on this wonderfully Bagnoldesque, slightly *roué demi-monde* of the understudy with its revered little "between-stairs" exactitudes—What was I saying?
Regina You were saying you weren't going to say it twice.
Known Actress Have I offended you or something dear? Is my coming in here somehow an unwarranted intrusion, because if it is I'm most awfully sorry but you're going to have to find some generous way of understanding that I am carrying a most monstrous responsibility, and I need your help—bless you darling. I'm not going to harp on about it because we have no time for rehearsal let alone the fiddliness of having to pull rank, and I am *not* pulling rank, Giles dear, so don't feel—look at me darling—that you have to look up to me. I've been in this business too long I assure you to want to contest that we are not all in the same storm-tossed boat, whether one is battling with the social niceties of the Captain's table, or rowing in the galley!

Pause

(*To Regina*) So will you hold me dear, here, and I'm going to *thrash*. Is that all right?
Regina Where are we going from?
Known Actress/Helen (*thrashing and strangling*) Come strangle—!
Charles I'm sorry Trixie doesn't strangle—
Known Actress I'm not strangling. I'm embracing. She's strangling.
Regina I've never strangled—
Known Actress Then could you try, dear, please, for me, or we'll never get anywhere? (*To Stella*) Sheila, dear, could you not knit, just for two seconds, darling? I know you're bored and resentful

Act II, Scene 4   47

and close to tears, but we are professionals. Whatever we're feeling, we have to look bright! That's what's so wonderful about actors. We smile through our tears. The show goes on through the storm, through the blitz, even if there's only *one* person there. We never close. We're like children. We get so excited! (*Sighs*) *I* do anyway. I'm like a schoolgirl, just arrived, don't know anyone, and I am probably going to make the most frightful hash of everything, but it's *my* life, *my* fate, that's strapped to the line—and we can't stop the train! Like Helen herself I am "a pearl cast upon the sweet dunghill of this age!" I *know* Helen. I know her stiffness, her frustration. I can feel the blood—clotting in her veins, in her old, sclerotic, varicose veins . . . She so wants to climb to the top of the steps but her poor old pins won't carry her. (*To Regina*) So you must hold me dear, constrict me, strangle me, embrace me, as I am embracing, and strangling you, my darling.

The embrace and strangle

Fake it, dear, fake it!—till magically we don't know who's strangling, who's embracing, like those wonderfully muscular wrestling statues by Michelangelo—(*To Stella*) is it Michelangelo?
Stella Stella.
Known Actress And that's the *pity* of it, because I *want* and *deserve* to be strangled but being Jove's daughter, I'm immortal, so can't be, whereas you *don't* want to be but *can* be, being only my *half*-sister. (*To Stella*) Correct me if I'm wrong darling, you look so unhappy!—our mother, after her encounter with the swan, having laid *two* eggs, out of one of which sprang Castor and dear Clytemnestra, previously fertilized by Tyndarus who was a mere mortal, and the other one, fertilized by Jove in his extraordinary manifestation as the swan, producing Helen herself and and and and and . . .
Stella Pollux.
Charles Should we break it for a moment there, loves?
Known Actress (*collapsing on the couch*) Oh, yes please, darling. I don't know about Helen and her immortality, but I am pooped.
Charles Shall I see you in the green room, loves?

Charles exits

Known Actress Retch, would it be too much trouble to ask you to procure for me just a glass or small bottle of pure plain uncarbonated water—?

Regina fills a mug from the sink and hands it to her

Thank you dear.

Regina goes

The Known Actress stops Stella

Darling I know what you're feeling: that I've barged in out of nowhere, robbing you of a lifetime's opportunity. It's true isn't it?
Stella Yes.
Known Actress When P.Q. took me to the Savoy and *begged* me over tea and scones to take this part, I said: But surely Trixie already *has* an understudy. And he said: Yes darling, but she wants the part *too much.* And I was about to say: Well, of course she does, you bastard, why else is she in the business? Then I remembered I'm in the business too, and *I* want this part, and to get the part you want darling, as I'm sure you're aware, you have to be prepared to kill for it!
Stella Yes.
Known Actress But that's no reason, my love, why we can't be friends.

Regina comes in with cups of tea for herself and Stella

Now I want you to tell me darlings, how I'm doing. Tell me the truth. Tell me I'm good.

Pause

I *am* good. I have to be. Helen was right. Oh yes I've met Helen. Years and years ago I met her at a fair, her ancient sun-baked corrugated face masking the beauty she once was, grey cataracts damming the wells of love in her sightless eyes. She told my fortune. She told me I would have to wait until the "autumn of my career" for that rise to the stars that we all crave, don't we darlings? And of course I didn't believe her—I was young, I was beautiful, I was just starting—and *because* I didn't believe her, I worked—my *God* how I worked—I hewed my career out of granite, just to spite her! I never rested, never. Even when I became "known" I didn't slacken for one moment. I still wrote the letters, and went to those awful parties, and yes I slept with people, I don't deny it, if I knew it would help, and it did. Oh yes darlings, it's the oldest profession in the world. It's not luck, dears, not even one per cent luck is it? It's

Act II, Scene 5

guile, charm, grit, obsession, and . . . (*with timing*) . . . timing. Oh my dears, you are enviable. You're sweet, I love you, for not *minding*. You don't mind, do you darlings, being *under* the stars, looking up, content to gaze . . .

Pause

Regina (*to Stella*) Trixie's going into hospital. On Wednesday. She'll be off for at least six weeks.
Known Actress What . . .?
Regina I heard P.Q. on the phone. No one's to know. Not even you. It mustn't get out.

Regina exits

Pause

Known Actress (*delving into her bag*) You've got to help me dear.
Stella With lines?
Known Actress No no, *letters*. (*She produces a stack of envelopes, filofax, reel of labels, pens*) Addresses—producers, casting directors, critics, friends, dear friends, dear friends of friends. They must all go out, first class, tonight.
Stella What must?
Known Actress (*producing a sheaf of copies*) I've run off rather an attractive little press release, like an invitation. Do you like it? Just fill in the date, whatever it is, next Wednesday . . .
Stella April the first.
Known Actress (*doing her lines*) For Helen it is fated she should walk the earth alone unshelter'd—Child of Man, wouldst thou could Godst—would thoust could—cod goodst thou wouldst . . .
Stella Would thou couldst God's child cheat of breath!
Known Actress I want to cut that line.

Black-out

Scene 5

Voices over the main speakers

Dame/Clytemnestra Thou art no child of God thou scarlet fiend!
Trixie/Helen Thou couldst so sweetly grant my long'd-for peace!

Dame/Clytemnestra I only cannot strangle thee because
         my hands are twisted, crabb'd with age—
Trixie/Helen   As mine
         dear sister!
Dame/Clytemnestra   I would wring thy neck—
Trixie/Helen   If I could—
Dame/Clytemnestra —if I could!
Trixie/Helen   —I'd thee embrace—
Dame/Clytemnestra   I stumbl'—!
Trixie/Helen I've caught thee!
Dame/Clytemnestra   Let me go!
Trixie/Helen   Let us ascend—
         crabb'd hand in crabb'd hand—
Dame/Clytemnestra   Let me climb alone—!

Voices fade as the Lights come up on the dressing-room. Regina is stuffing and licking envelopes. Stella is quietly packing

Stella What are you doing this for?
Regina I'm doing it for her. I want her to have a full house.
Stella But she won't be on.
Regina Won't she?
Stella Trixie isn't going into hospital.
Regina Isn't she?
Stella You know she isn't. Not on Wednesday.
Regina Then what am I doing this for?
Stella It's a trick.
Regina A trick?
Stella Wednesday is April the first.
Regina Oh I see!
Stella You're not really going to—?
Regina Post them? Yes.
Stella But what if they all come? You're going to make an absolute fool of her.
Regina I'm going to make an absolute fool of her.
Stella But that's terrible!
Regina It's theatre.
Stella It is not theatre.
Regina It's revenge.
Stella It's petty.
Regina Revenge is petty.

Act II, Scene 5

Stella I know I'm old-fashioned but I believe in ideals, the great dramas, giving people something exquisite and shining to yearn for.
Regina You mean TV commercials.
Stella It's no use talking to you Regina. You've no conception of great drama.
Regina Great drama, Stella, is about selfishly getting your own back.
Stella What absolute rot!
Regina In the most vicious way possible.
Stella (*collecting her things*) I can't stay in the same room as you.
Regina Gouging out an eye for an eye, demanding pounds of flesh, making an absolute fool of people.
Stella Just when I thought we were getting on.
Regina *King Lear, Merchant of Venice, Twelfth Night—*
Stella Go on, reel them off! You're the great actress!
Regina *The Oresteia, Measure for Measure, School for Scandal, Charley's Aunt* . . .
Stella *Macbeth*. (*Pause*) Macbeth Macbeth Macbeth . . .
Regina Don't say that. Stop it.
Stella Beware the Thane of Fife!
Regina Not in here.
Stella Dismiss me. Enough!

Pause

You're not superstitious.
Regina No, but you are.
Stella Not any more. I'm leaving.

Pause

Regina You'll miss my Jubilee. Next Wednesday. We're having a party. Everyone's coming. Trixie, the Dame, P.Q. . . .
Stella It's not true.
Regina It's not true.
Stella The show's closing anyway. He told me. I asked him and he said it wasn't, most emphatically. So it must be.
Regina You're getting cynical dear, which is bad, which means good. Let's not say good-bye.
Stella Good-bye.

Stella goes

Regina Good-bye.

Lights fade to Black-out

SCENE 6

Tannoy This is your half an hour call. Half an hour please, ladies and gentlemen.

Charles is in a solo spot, on the phone

Charles Stella . . .? Stella, it's Charles . . . (*He laughs*) How are you love . . .? That's great because you see, we want you back . . . We do, we're desperate . . . No, I mean we want you to drop everything, and come *now* . . . It's after the half and we've had a calamity . . . No not Trixie, she's fine . . . It's the "Known Actress". Remember her? Well you can forget her. She's done a bunk and we want you, we all want you. P.Q. especially, he was asking for you, and he has so much on his mind, because you were not far wrong Stella, about (*whispering*) closing . . . It's more than a whisper, it's a rumour, and the only reason we're nearly half full tonight, is the K.A.'s indefatigable self-publicity! How does anyone *know* so many people! She was *bussing* them in! It was her Royal Command Performance, it really was! And when she wasn't on the phone, she was doing movement and voice, going over and over her scenes with the Dame and doing lines with Reg. And there was an *invasion* of cards and flowers and prezzies from friends and admirers which she would *not* be distracted by. She needed one hour she said, to "find Helen" in Trixie's dressing-room, can you believe, and do her face, get into costume. Now you're wondering, we all were—what *was* going on? What had happened to Trixie? I'll tell you—nothing! Nothing at all! She turned up, on the half, coughing and crotchety as ever—I was there, I saw it all, I was just passing her dressing-room and the door was ajar and I could see this figure, ensconced, the spitting image of Trixie! Honestly, I tried to warn her, but Trixie she's like an eel when she wants to be. She beat me to it. She slipped in and I saw her just standing there, fuming you could tell, but she's pro enough not to show it. She said: "I think, my dear, you've strayed into the wrong room. Would you kindly *fuck off* please?"

Spot snaps off on Charles

Scene 7

A performance is in progress. Voices are heard on the main speakers

Trixie/Helen Here now breathless at last we stand before this door of death.
Regina/Clytemnestra Behind which welcome portal doth my son await justly to slay his mother for her crimes.
Trixie/Helen Let us then both go in that he may bag a brace of sisters—
Regina/Clytemnestra But the Fates have not decreed—
Trixie/Helen Who needs the Fates?
Regina/Clytemnestra —that swift relief—
Trixie/Helen Let's cheat the hags!
Regina/Clytemnestra —should greet the harlot Helen.

The Voices fade down

Lights up on the dressing-room, filled to overflowing with huge bouquets of spring flowers

Stella comes in with a small bunch of daffodils still in bud. She looks around, amazed at the array of flowers

Stella Regina . . .? Reg . . .? (*She looks for her*) Is this one of your tricks . . .?

Charles comes in

Charles Stella, thank God you've come!
Stella Charles, what's happening? Is it the Jubilee?
Charles You're not going to believe this, Stella love.
Stella I would have been here sooner but I wanted to get some . . . flowers . . .

Charles Sit down a minute . . .
Stella (*amazed*) Where did they all come from?
Charles What?
Stella The flowers.
Charles Oh, they're nothing. They were the K.A.'s.
Stella Oh. I thought they were for . . . Reg . . . (*She looks down at her flowers*) I wanted to get some which hadn't come out yet, so they might last . . .
Charles (*turning up the tannoy*) Listen.
Regina/Clytemnestra My sorrowing son hath but one mother, but one
    murd'rous mother, who with her fell axe
    did fell the tree . . .
Stella It's Regina . . .! She's *on* . . .!
Regina/Clytemnestra   Now must those fatal branches
    fall on my head only. *My* son must
    alone my eyelids close . . .
Stella She's wonderful! On her Jubilee!
Regina/Clytemnestra   . . . and reaching deep
    into the flesh that bore him, drench me with
    his tears, that I in death may birth a second
    son to rise aveng'd and purg'd . . .

The performance continues under the following

Stella I'm going out front. I'm going to cheer—
Charles She's only doing the fall, then the Dame's going back on.
Stella (*appalled*) Why?
Charles She sprained her ankle. It's not serious. She's just not doing the fall.
Stella I'll sprain the other one! I'll mangle it! She *can't* go back on . . .
Trixie/Helen   But sister
    I'm the cause—
Regina/Clytemnestra   This is my moment, mine!
    Thy painted face my son shall never see!
Trixie/Helen See me he shall!
Regina/Clytemnestra   Not if these ancient hands—
Trixie/Helen —if first these ancient hands—
Regina/Clytemnestra   —can first scratch out
    thine eyes!

Act II, Scene 7   55

Trixie/Helen (*blinded*) Mine eyes!
Regina/Clytemnestra   Come out thou cyst! And thou!
Trixie/Helen Don't blind me!
Regina/Clytemnestra   Eyes that launched a thousand ships
          be dash'd!
Trixie/Helen   Ah me!
Regina/Clytemnestra   And dash'd again!
Trixie/Helen   Ah woe!
Stella I think she's *better* than the Dame.
Charles She's certainly stronger on the blinding.

The performance is continuing

Regina/Clytemnestra Now is my long'd-for fatal moment come.
Trixie/Helen My eyes cast out can see thy heel come down . . .
Regina/Clytemnestra I reach and lift the latch—
Trixie/Helen   —and happ'n to tread
          on my soft orb—
Regina/Clytemnestra   I slip—
Trixie/Helen   —on tears!
Regina/Clytemnestra   Help me!
Trixie/Helen Oh I'll help thee!
Regina/Clytemnestra   Steady me—
Trixie/Helen   Fly—
Regina/Clytemnestra   Forgive me—
Trixie/Helen —down the staaaaaaaaaairs . . .!
Regina/Clytemnestra Aaaaaaaaaaaaaaaagh . . .!!

Silence

Charles Trixie's in the pin-spot now, so the Dame and Reg can swap places.
Stella It's so unfair!
Charles We're hoping no one will have noticed.
Stella She's a star. She must be seen.
Dame/Clytemnestra Ah me! I live! I am condemn'd to life!
Charles (*with relief*) The Dame's back. They didn't notice!
Trixie/Helen Live on absolved. All thy guilt be mine.
          I die for thee—
Dame/Clytemnestra   Ah woe on woe! For now
          thy blinding and thy death shall weigh on me!

Trixie/Helen *Thou* art Jove's daughter, *thou* his true belov'd,
  who yearnedst only to be wife and mother . . .
Dame/Clytemnestra How can I be wife to him I killed
  and mother to a son who must avenge—?
Trixie/Helen & Stella Time shall teach thy heart this door of death,
  should be kept clos'd, and shunn'd should be the magic
  wild boundless unknown. And time shall teach
  thy soul to rest content within those old
  familiar dark'ning walls where fires still glow
  and clocks still chime the hours . . .

Charles turns the tannoy down

The door bursts open. Regina enters, in magnificent black and gold costume, made up as Clytemnestra

Stella Regina . . .
Charles Well done, Reg.
Stella Regina you were magic, magnificent.

Regina comes in to the chair, limping slightly

Regina All in a day's work. (*She removes her head-dress, kicks off her stack shoes*)
Stella Oh no. This was special.
Charles Do you like the costume?
Stella Your Silver Jubilee . . .
Charles Amazing what wardrobe can cobble together. What is this "jubilee"?
Regina I don't know. Something Stella dreamt up.
Stella She's been understudying the Dame for exactly twenty-five years and this is the first time she's been on!
Regina What do you mean? I've been on dozens of times!
Stella (*laughing*) Regina I don't know when to believe you. Don't take your make-up off! You've got the curtain call.
Charles I don't think she needs—
Stella Oh, but she must, she must.
Regina I can't.
Stella Of course you can!
Regina I don't have a shawl. (*Mimicking Stella*) A shawl, a shawl, my kingdom for a shawl!
Charles Reg, you are magnificent.

Act II, Scene 7

Stella I'm going out front. I'm going to stand in the audience. They'll be clamouring!
Charles They may not have noticed.
Stella I'll *make* them notice! I'm going to clap till I burst! (*Running out*) I'm going to shout for you till you're forced to come on . . .

Stella exits

Charles I hope she doesn't. The Dame would go bananas.

Regina isn't taking her make-up off

You don't really want to . . .?
Regina I don't know.

Pause

Charles You couldn't . . . without the Dame's permission.
Regina Go and ask her.
Charles But she's on stage.
Regina As soon as she comes off. There's a moment before the curtain, just ask her if she wouldn't mind . . .
Tannoy Stand by please for lights down on Act Three.
Regina (*putting on her head-dress and stack shoes*) Go on. Hurry!
Charles We'll call you over the tannoy.

Charles exits

Tannoy Stand by full company for curtain call.

Regina turns up the tannoy. Waits. Sudden roar of applause. It continues for several minutes. Regina stays motionless, then removes the head-dress and shoes. She looks at the bouquets of flowers. Goes round collecting them all up, as the applause continues and bins them in the dustbin and draws the curtain. When the room is clear, she starts taking her make-up off. The applause subsides until at last only one pair of hands is frantically clapping. Stella's voice can be heard

Stella (*over tannoy, yelling from the back of the auditorium*) Understudy! Understudy! Understudy! Understudy! Understudy . . .!

Silence

Regina wipes her face clean

Stella comes in

Stella You didn't take the call.
Regina I knew I'd forgotten something!
Stella (*close to tears*) It was your Jubilee, and no one noticed.
Regina Sleight of hand.
Stella The Dame should have dragged you on.
Regina I didn't have a shawl.
Stella God, she's a bitch. I suppose she didn't even drop by to say thank you.
Regina She did actually.
Stella She didn't.
Regina She did.
Stella She did not.
Regina She did! (*Pause*) She tapped on the door. I said "Come in". She peeped round. She was really sweet. She said she'd come to thank me not only for tonight, but for twenty-five years' faithful service.
Stella She remembered?
Regina She even kissed me. She gave me this.
Stella What is it?
Regina A present.
Stella Where?
Regina I'm miming it.

Pause

Tannoy Just to remind you, there'll be an understudies' rehearsal, tomorrow ten o'clock. Good night.
Stella Where have all the flowers gone?

Pause

Shouldn't you be getting changed? Regina . . .?

Regina gets changed

Regina Did I tell you about my nephew?
Stella The one who's a bassoonist?
Regina He's more than just a bassoonist.
Stella (*putting on her coat*) What's he doing now?
Regina Well, you know he used to be in a symphony orchestra. Poor love he just couldn't make ends meet. And he's so ambitious.

Stella It doesn't do to be too ambitious.
Regina Well fortunately, he got a job in the band for a West End show.
Stella That was lucky.
Regina (*putting her coat on*) Though he knew it wouldn't last.
Stella Well, they don't.
Regina And it didn't. (*She puts the lights out and starts to go*) Well you'll never guess.
Stella What?
Regina We just heard the other day he's finally made it into playing jingles . . .

Stella and Regina leave the dressing room

Stella (*distantly*) Jingles . . .?
Regina You know TV commercials . . .

The Lights fade

CURTAIN

FURNITURE AND PROPERTY LIST

Further dressing may be added at the director's discretion

ACT I

Scene 1

On stage: Mirror framed with light bulbs, cards, photos, etc.
Dressing table. *On it:* magazines, kettle and mugs, knitting, shopping bags, make-up box
Chipped basin with practical taps
Costume rail
Folding screen and curtain
Dustbin
Old easy chair. *On it:* cushion
Folding chairs
Chaise-longue
Phone
Tannoy

Personal: **Charles:** stop-watch, book

Scene 2

Personal: **Regina:** mohair shawl knitting

Scene 3

Set: Knife

Off stage: Carrier bags. In them: food, a melon (**Regina**)
Red costume (**Charles**)

Scene 4

Personal: **Charles:** book
Regina: completed shawl

SCENE 5

Personal: **Regina:** new shawl knitting

ACT II

SCENE 1

Personal: P.Q.: pocket phone

SCENE 2

Set: Bag. *In it:* food

SCENE 3

Set: Blood capsules behind easy chair

SCENE 4

Personal: **Known Actress:** script. Hand bag. *In it:* evelopes, filofax, reel of labels, pens, sheaf of copies
Charles: book

SCENE 5

On stage: Leaflets and envelopes

SCENE 7

Set: Bouquets of spring flowers

Off stage: Bunch of daffodils (**Stella**)

LIGHTING PLOT

Property fittings required: nil.
Practical fittings required: mirror framed by light bulbs
Interior. The same throughout

ACT I, SCENE 1

To open: Two spots on **Stella** and **Regina**, general lighting, gradually increasing

| Cue 1 | **Stella/Helen:** ". . . stiff-neck'd sister's heart."
Fade to Black-out | (Page 7) |

ACT I, SCENE 2

To open: Black-out

| Cue 2 | **Dame/Clytemnestra:** ". . . in thine accurs'd adult'rous fires . . .!
Bring up general lighting | (Page 8) |
| Cue 3 | **Regina:** ". . . Sainsbury's tomorrow morning."
Fade to Black-out | (Page 15) |

ACT I, SCENE 3

To open: General lighting

| Cue 4 | **Stella:** ". . . he was so tired . . ."
Fade to Black-out | (Page 22) |

ACT I, SCENE 4

To open: Black-out

| Cue 5 | **Trixie's** voice fades
Bring up general lighting | (Page 22) |
| Cue 6 | **Regina:** . . . and a carrot . . ."
Fade to Black-out | (Page 25) |

Under the Stars

ACT I, SCENE 5

To open: General lighting

No cues

ACT II, SCENE 1

To open: General lighting

| Cue 7 | **Regina:** ". . . murderer's breast . . ."
 Fade to Black-out | (Page 35) |

ACT II, SCENE 2

To open: Black-out

| Cue 8 | As voices fade
 Bring up general lighting | (Page 36) |
| Cue 9 | **Charles:** "He wants to see you."
 Black-out | (Page 39) |

ACT II, SCENE 3

To open: General lighting

| Cue 10 | **Stella:** ". . . and over and out . . ."
 Fade to Black-out | (Page 44) |

ACT II, SCENE 4

To open: Black-out

| Cue 11 | As voices fade
 Bring up general lighting | (Page 44) |
| Cue 12 | **Known Actress:** ". . . cut that line."
 Black-out | (Page 49) |

ACT II, SCENE 5

To open: Black-out

| Cue 13 | **Dame/Clytemnestra:** "Let me climb alone—!"
 Bring up general lighting | (Page 50) |
| Cue 14 | **Regina:** "Good-bye".
 Fade to Black-out | (Page 52) |

ACT II, SCENE 6

To open: Black-out

Cue 15	**Tannoy:** ". . . please, ladies and gentlemen." *Spot on Charles*	(Page 52)
Cue 16	**Charles:** ". . . fuck off please?" *Cut spot on Charles*	(Page 53)

ACT II, SCENE 7

To open: Black-out

Cue 17	As voices fade down *Bring up general lighting*	(Page 53)
Cue 18	**Regina:** "You know TV commercials . . ." *Fade to Black-out*	(Page 59)

EFFECTS PLOT

ACT I

Cue 1	**Charles:** ". . . will have to be amended . . ." Tannoy Announcement *as script page 7*	(Page 7)
Cue 2	To open Scene 2 *Voices of* **Trixie** *and* **The Dame** *over front-of-house speakers as script page 8*	(Page 8)
Cue 3	Lights come up *Voices of* **Trixie** *and* **The Dame** *switch to the tannoy*	(Page 8)
Cue 4	**Regina** turns the tannoy down *Fade down voices of* **Trixie** *and* **The Dame**	(Page 8)
Cue 5	**Stella:** "I won't shorten it." Pause Tannoy Announcement *as script page 12*	(Page 12)
Cue 6	**Regina:** "But bitch eats bitch." Tannoy Announcement *as script page 13*	(Page 13)
Cue 7	**Regina** cuts the melon karate-style Tannoy Announcement *as script page 15*	(Page 15)
Cue 8	**Regina:** "You really have done it now, Charles . . ." Tannoy Announcement *as script page 19*	(Page 19)
Cue 9	**Stella:** "Seventeen." Tannoy Announcement *as script page 22*	(Page 21)
Cue 10	To open Scene 4 **Trixie's** *voice over front-of-house speakers as script page 22*	(Page 22)
Cue 11	**Stella** turns up the tannoy **Trixie's** *and* **The Dame's** *voices over tannoy as script page 26*	(Page 26)
Cue 12	**Stella** turns down the tannoy *Fade down the tannoy as script page 26*	(Page 26)
Cue 13	**Regina:** ". . . the murderer's gibbet . . ." Tannoy Announcement *as script page 28*	(Page 28)
Cue 14	**Charles:** ". . . They're waiting . . ." Pause Tannoy Announcement *as script page 29*	(Page 28)

Cue 15	**Stella:** "Thank you, Charles . . ." **Tannoy Announcement** *as script page 29*	(Page 29)
Cue 16	**Stella:** ". . . play older than I really am . . ." *Voices of* **Trixie** *and* **The Dame** *as script page 29*	(Page 29)

ACT II

Cue 17	To open Scene 2 *Voices over front-of-house speakers as script page 35*	(Page 35)
Cue 18	**Regina:** "We'll be out soon enough." **Tannoy Announcement** *as script page 39*	(Page 39)
Cue 19	**Regina:** "Oh dear." **Tannoy Announcement** *as script page 39*	(Page 39)
Cue 20	To open Scene 4 *Voices over front-of-house speakers as script page 44*	(Page 45)
Cue 21	To open Scene 5 *Voices over front-of-house speakers as script page 49*	(Page 49)
Cue 22	To open Scene 6 **Tannoy** *as script page 52*	(Page 52)
Cue 23	To open Scene 7 *Voices over front-of-house speakers as script page 53*	(Page 53)
Cue 24	**Charles** turns up the tannoy *Voices over the tannoy as script page 54*	(Page 54)
Cue 25	**Charles** turns down the tannoy *Fade down the tannoy*	(Page 56)
Cue 26	**Regina:** ". . . just ask her if she wouldn't mind . . ." **Tannoy** *as script page 57*	(Page 57)
Cue 27	**Charles** exits **Tannoy** *as script page 57*	(Page 57)
Cue 28	**Regina** turns up the tannoy **Stella's** *voice on the tannoy as script page 57*	(Page 57)
Cue 29	**Regina:** "I'm miming it." Pause **Tannoy** *as script page 58*	(Page 58)

PRINTED IN GREAT BRITAIN BY
THE LONGDUNN PRESS LTD., BRISTOL.

www.ingramcontent.com/pod-product-compliance
Ingram Content Group UK Ltd.
Pitfield, Milton Keynes, MK11 3LW, UK
UKHW021846210426
5322IPUK00022B/504